The Young Baptist's Catechism

The Young Baptist's Catechism

A Beginner's Guide to the Baptist Confession of Faith of 1689

ADAM MURRELL

Resource *Publications*

An imprint of *Wipf and Stock Publishers*
199 West 8th Avenue • Eugene OR 97401

THE YOUNG BAPTIST'S CATECHISM
A Beginner's Guide to the Baptist Confession of Faith of 1689

ISBN 13: 978-1-55635-261-4

Manufactured in the U.S.A.

For Rylee, Emily, and Elizabeth

Note to the Reader

[4]Hear, O Israel! The Lord is our God, the Lord is one! [5]You shall love the Lord your God with all your heart and with all your soul and with all your might. [6]These words, which I am commanding you today, shall be on your heart. [7]You shall teach them diligently to your sons and shall talk of them when you sit in your house and when you walk by the way and when you lie down and when you rise up (Deut 6:4–7).

One of the greatest gifts parents can give their children is a godly education. Instruction in righteousness is not only necessary for good order and discipline, it is commanded by God. Deuteronomy 6:4–7 records the earnestness of forming a child's character. Every Christian parent should embrace his God-given responsibility to train up a child for the glory of God. It is for His kingdom that we should strive to bring up our children in the training and admonition of the Lord. And one of the best ways to accomplish this is through the constant and consistent training of children in what is right and proper. But how can this be effectively accomplished? One way is to develop a fundamental understanding of God and His word through the exercise of catechizing. This instructional method of asking questions and receiving answers is an often overlooked form of instructing. But there is seldom a better tool for introducing young people to Christian truths than to use a catechism. My starting point (other than the Bible) was the London Baptist Confession of Faith of 1689. It has been my chief aim to prepare a summation of that confession and to transform it into a catechism for both children and adults. I pray that you will find this beneficial in your pursuit to know God and to teach others about Him.

Adam Murrell
February 2007
Pascagoula, Mississippi

Question 1. Who is the first and greatest of all beings?

Answer: God is the first *(a)* and greatest of all beings *(b) (c)*.

Scripture: Isa 44:6; Ps 8:1, 97:9

(a) Thus says the Lord, the King of Israel and his Redeemer, the Lord of hosts: 'I am the first and I am the last, And there is no God besides Me. (Isa 44:6)

(b) O Lord, our Lord, How majestic is Your name in all the earth, Who have displayed Your splendor above the heavens! (Ps 8:1)

(c) For You are the Lord Most High over all the earth; You are exalted far above all gods. (Ps 97:9)

Question 2. How do we know God exists?

Answer: God reveals Himself to us *(a) (b) (c)*.

Scripture: Ps 19:1–2, Rom 1:18–20, 1 Cor 2:9–10

(a) ¹The heavens are telling of the glory of God; And their expanse is declaring the work of His hands. ²Day to day pours forth speech, And night to night reveals knowledge. (Ps 19:1–2)

(b) ¹⁸For the wrath of God is revealed from heaven against all ungodliness and unrighteousness of men who suppress the truth in unrighteousness, ¹⁹because that which is known about God is evident within them; for God made it evident to them. ²⁰For since the creation of the world His invisible attributes, His eternal power and divine nature, have been clearly seen, being understood through what has been made, so that they are without excuse. (Rom 1:18–20)

(c) ⁹but just as it is written, "THINGS WHICH EYE HAS NOT SEEN AND EAR HAS NOT HEARD, AND WHICH HAVE NOT ENTERED THE HEART OF MAN, ALL THAT GOD HAS PREPARED FOR

THOSE WHO LOVE HIM." [10]For to us God revealed them through the Spirit; for the Spirit searches all things, even the depths of God. (1 Cor 2:9–10)

Question 3. How does He reveal himself to us?

Answer: God reveals Himself through nature *(a)*, the Bible *(b)*, and Jesus Christ *(c)*.

Scripture: Ps 19:1–2, 2 Tim 3:16, John 1:1

(a) [1]The heavens are telling of the glory of God; And their expanse is declaring the work of His hands. [2]Day to day pours forth speech, And night to night reveals knowledge. (Ps 19:1–2)

(b) All Scripture is inspired by God and profitable for teaching, for reproof, for correction, for training in righteousness. (2 Tim 3:16)

(c) In the beginning was the Word, and the Word was with God, and the Word was God. (John 1:1)

Question 4. Who made you?

Answer: God made me *(a) (b)*.

Scripture: Ps 139:13, Jer 1:5

(a) For You formed my inward parts; You wove me in my mother's womb. (Ps 139:13)

(b) Before I formed you in the womb I knew you, And before you were born I consecrated you; I have appointed you a prophet to the nations. (Jer 1:5)

Question 5. What other things did God make?

Answer: God made everything *(a) (b)*.

Scripture: Gen 1:1, Ps 89:11

(a) In the beginning God created the heavens and the earth. (Gen 1:1)

(b) The heavens are Yours, the earth also is Yours; The world and all it contains, You have founded them. (Ps 89:11)

Question 6. Who made God?

Answer: No one made God, He is eternal *(a) (b) (c) (d)*.

Scripture: Ps 90:2, Isa 41:4, 1 Tim 1:17, Rev 22:13

(a) Before the mountains were born or You gave birth to the earth and the world, Even from everlasting to everlasting, You are God. (Ps 90:2)

(b) Who has performed and accomplished it, calling forth the generations from the beginning? I, the LORD, am the first, and with the last I am He. (Isa 41:4)

(c) Now to the King eternal, immortal, invisible, the only God, be honor and glory forever and ever. Amen. (1 Tim 1:17)

(d) I am the Alpha and the Omega, the first and the last, the beginning and the end. (Rev 22:13)

Question 7. What is God?

Answer: God is spirit *(a)*, infinite *(b)*, unchanging *(c)*, powerful *(d)*, perfect in his being, displaying compassion, and loving kindness *(e)*.

Scripture: John 4:24, Job 11:7, Jas 1:17, Ps 147:5, Exod 34:6, 7

(a) God is spirit, and those who worship Him must worship in spirit and truth. (John 4:24)

(b) Can you discover the depths of God? Can you discover the limits of the Almighty? (Job 11:7)

(c) Every good thing given and every perfect gift is from above, coming down from the Father of lights, with whom there is no variation or shifting shadow. (Jas 1:17)

(d) Great is our Lord and abundant in strength; His understanding is infinite. (Ps 147:5)

(e) ⁶Then the LORD passed by in front of him and proclaimed, "The LORD, the LORD God, compassionate and gracious, slow to anger, and abounding in loving kindness and truth; ⁷who keeps loving kindness for thousands, who forgives iniquity, transgression and sin; yet He will by no means leave the guilty unpunished, visiting the iniquity of fathers on the children and on the grandchildren to the third and fourth generations." (Exod 34:6–7)

Question 8. Is there more than one God?

Answer: The Lord is the only God *(a)*, the true and living One *(b)*.

Scripture: Deut 4:35, Jer 10:10

(a) To you it was shown that you might know that the LORD, He is God; there is no other besides Him. (Deut 4:35)

(b) But the LORD is the true God; He is the living God and the everlasting King At His wrath the earth quakes, And the nations cannot endure His indignation. (Jer 10:10)

Question 9. How many persons are there in the Godhead?

Answer: There are three persons in the Godhead *(a) (b)*, equal in power and glory *(c) (d) (e)*.

Scripture: 1 John 5:7, 1 Cor 8:6, John 10:30, Acts 5:3–4, 2 Cor 13:14

(a) For there are three that testify. (1 John 5:7)

(b) Yet for us there is but one God, the Father, from whom are all things and we exist for Him; and one Lord, Jesus Christ, by whom are all things, and we exist through Him. (1 Cor 8:6)

(c) I and the Father are one. (John 10:30)

(d) [3]But Peter said, "Ananias, why has Satan filled your heart to lie to the Holy Spirit and to keep back some of the price of the land? [4]"While it remained unsold, did it not remain your own? And after it was sold, was it not under your control? Why is it that you have conceived this deed in your heart? You have not lied to men but to God." (Acts 5:3–4)

(e) The grace of the Lord Jesus Christ, and the love of God, and the fellowship of the Holy Spirit, be with you all. (2 Cor 13:14)

Question 10. Who are the three persons in the Godhead?

Answer: The three persons in the Godhead *(a)* are God the Father, God the Son, and God the Holy Spirit *(b) (c)*.

Scripture: 1 John 5:7, Matt 28:19, 2 Cor 13:14

(a) For there are three that testify. (1 John 5:7)

(b) Go therefore and make disciples of all the nations, baptizing them in the name of the Father and the Son and the Holy Spirit. (Matt 28:19)

(c) The grace of the Lord Jesus Christ, and the love of God, and the fellowship of the Holy Spirit, be with you all. (2 Cor 13:14)

Question 11.   What does God the Father do in salvation?

Answer: God the Father chooses His people *(a) (b) (c) (d) (e)*.

Scripture: John 6:37–40, 65, Rom 8:29–30, Rom 9:14–23, Eph 1:3–6

(a) ³⁷All that the Father gives Me will come to Me, and the one who comes to Me I will certainly not cast out. ³⁸For I have come down from heaven, not to do My own will, but the will of Him who sent Me. ³⁹This is the will of Him who sent Me, that of all that He has given Me I lose nothing, but raise it up on the last day. ⁴⁰For this is the will of My Father, that everyone who beholds the Son and believes in Him will have eternal life, and I Myself will raise him up on the last day. (John 6:37–40)

(b) And He was saying, "For this reason I have said to you, that no one can come to Me unless it has been granted him from the Father." (John 6:65)

(c) ²⁹For those whom He foreknew, He also predestined to become conformed to the image of His Son, so that He would be the firstborn among many brethren; ³⁰and these whom He predestined, He also called; and these whom He called, He also justified; and these whom He justified, He also glorified. (Rom 8:29–30)

(d) ¹⁴What shall we say then? There is no injustice with God, is there? May it never be! ¹⁵For He says to Moses, "I WILL HAVE MERCY ON WHOM I HAVE MERCY, AND I WILL HAVE

COMPASSION ON WHOM I HAVE COMPASSION." [16]So then it does not depend on the man who wills or the man who runs, but on God who has mercy. [17]For the Scripture says to Pharaoh, "FOR THIS VERY PURPOSE I RAISED YOU UP, TO DEMONSTRATE MY POWER IN YOU, AND THAT MY NAME MIGHT BE PROCLAIMED THROUGHOUT THE WHOLE EARTH." [18]So then He has mercy on whom He desires, and He hardens whom He desires. [19]You will say to me then, "Why does He still find fault? For who resists His will?" [20]On the contrary, who are you, O man, who answers back to God? The thing molded will not say to the molder, "Why did you make me like this," will it? [21]Or does not the potter have a right over the clay, to make from the same lump one vessel for honorable use and another for common use? [22]What if God, although willing to demonstrate His wrath and to make His power known, endured with much patience vessels of wrath prepared for destruction? [23]And He did so to make known the riches of His glory upon vessels of mercy, which He prepared beforehand for glory. (Rom 9:14–23)

(e) [3]Blessed be the God and Father of our Lord Jesus Christ, who has blessed us with every spiritual blessing in the heavenly places in Christ, [4]just as He chose us in Him before the foundation of the world, that we would be holy and blameless before Him In love [5]He predestined us to adoption as sons through Jesus Christ to Himself, according to the kind intention of His will, [6]to the praise of the glory of His grace, which He freely bestowed on us in the Beloved. (Eph 1:3–6)

Question 12. What does Jesus do in salvation?

Answer: Jesus redeems (a) His people (b).

Scripture: Gal 2:16, Matt 1:21

(a) Nevertheless knowing that a man is not justified by the works of the Law but through faith in Christ Jesus, even we have believed in Christ Jesus, so that we may be justified by

faith in Christ and not by the works of the Law; since by
the works of the Law no flesh will be justified. (Gal 2:16)

(b) She will bear a Son; and you shall call His name Jesus, for
He will save His people from their sins. (Matt 1:21)

Question 13.   What does the Holy Spirit do in salvation?

Answer: The Holy Spirit quickens God's chosen people
(a).

Scripture: Titus 3:5–6

(a) [5]He saved us, not on the basis of deeds which we have
done in righteousness, but according to His mercy, by the
washing of regeneration and renewing by the Holy Spirit,
[6]whom He poured out upon us richly through Jesus Christ
our Savior. (Titus 3:5–6)

Question 14.   Why did He make all things?

Answer: God made all things for His glory and good pleasure *(a)*.

Scripture: Rev 4:11

(a) Worthy are You, our Lord and our God, to receive glory
and honor and power; for You created all things, and because of Your will they existed, and were created. (Rev 4:11)

Question 15.   How were things made?

Answer: God spoke and it came to be *(a)*.

Scripture: Gen 1:3–5

(a) [3]And God said, "Let there be light," and there was light.
[4]God saw that the light was good, and He separated the
light from the darkness. [5]God called the light "day," and

the darkness he called "night." And there was evening, and there was morning—the first day. (Gen 1:3–5)

Question 16. What is God's word?

Answer: The Bible is God's word *(a)*.

Scripture: 2 Tim 3:16

(a) All Scripture is inspired by God and profitable for teaching, for reproof, for correction, for training in righteousness. (2 Tim 3:16)

Question 17. What does the Bible primarily teach?

Answer: The Bible primarily teaches what man is to believe about God *(a)*.

Scripture: John 20:31

(a) But these have been written so that you may believe that Jesus is the Christ, the Son of God; and that believing you may have life in His name. (John 20:31)

Question 18. For whom was the Bible written?

Answer: The Bible was written for everyone *(a)*.

Scripture: Gal 3:24

(a) Therefore the Law has become our tutor to lead us to Christ, so that we may be justified by faith. (Gal 3:24)

Question 19. What does the Bible say God made on the first day?

Answer: On the first day, God made the light, and called it 'day' and the darkness He called 'night' *(a)*.

Scripture: Gen 1:3–5

(a) [3]ThenGod said, "Let there be light"; and there was light. [4]God saw that the light was good; and God separated the light from the darkness. [5]God called the light day, and the darkness He called night And there was evening and there was morning, one day. (Gen 1:3–5)

Question 20. What does the Bible say God made on the second day?

Answer: On the second day, God formed the clouds and skies *(a)*.

Scripture: Gen 1:6–8

(a) [6]Then God said, "Let there be an expanse in the midst of the waters, and let it separate the waters from the waters." [7]God made the expanse, and separated the waters which were below the expanse from the waters which were above the expanse; and it was so. [8]God called the expanse heaven. And there was evening and there was morning, a second day. (Gen 1:6–8)

Question 21. What does the Bible say God made on the third day?

Answer: On the third day, God created seas, land and vegetation *(a)*.

Scripture: Gen 1:9–13

(a) [9]Then God said, "Let the waters below the heavens be gathered into one place, and let the dry land appear"; and it was so. [10]God called the dry land earth, and the gathering of the waters He called seas; and God saw that it was good. [11]Then God said, "Let the earth sprout vegetation, plants yielding seed, and fruit trees on the earth bearing fruit after their kind with seed in them"; and it was so. [12]The earth brought forth vegetation, plants yielding seed after their kind, and trees bearing fruit with seed in them, after their kind; and God saw that it was good. [13]There was evening and there was morning, a third day. (Gen 1:9–13)

Question 22. What does the Bible say God made on the fourth day?

Answer: On the fourth day, God made the sun, moon and stars *(a)*.

Scripture: Gen 1:14–19

(a) [14]Then God said, "Let there be lights in the expanse of the heavens to separate the day from the night, and let them be for signs and for seasons and for days and years; [15]and let them be for lights in the expanse of the heavens to give light on the earth"; and it was so. [16]God made the two great lights, the greater light to govern the day, and the lesser light to govern the night; He made the stars also. [17]God placed them in the expanse of the heavens to give light on the earth, [18]and to govern the day and the night, and to separate the light from the darkness; and God saw that it

was good. [19]There was evening and there was morning, a fourth day. (Gen 1:14–19)

Question 23. What does the Bible say God made on the fifth day?

Answer: On the fifth day, God made the birds of the air and the fish of the sea *(a)*.

Scripture: Gen 1:20–23

(a) [20]Then God said, "Let the waters teem with swarms of living creatures, and let birds fly above the earth in the open expanse of the heavens." [21]God created the great sea monsters and every living creature that moves, with which the waters swarmed after their kind, and every winged bird after its kind; and God saw that it was good. [22]God blessed them, saying, "Be fruitful and multiply, and fill the waters in the seas, and let birds multiply on the earth." [23]There was evening and there was morning, a fifth day. (Gen 1:20–23)

Question 24. What does the Bible say God made on the sixth day?

Answer: On the sixth day, God made animals and created man to have dominion over them *(a)*.

Scripture: Gen 1:24–31

(a) [24]Then God said, "Let the earth bring forth living creatures after their kind: cattle and creeping things and beasts of the earth after their kind"; and it was so. [25]God made the beasts of the earth after their kind, and the cattle after their kind, and everything that creeps on the ground after its kind; and God saw that it was good. [26]Then God said, "Let Us make man in Our image, according to Our likeness; and let them rule over the fish of the sea and over the birds of the sky and over the cattle and over all the earth, and over every creeping thing that creeps on the earth." [27]God created man in His own image, in the image of God He created him; male and female He created them. [28]God blessed them; and God said to them, "Be fruitful and multiply, and fill the earth, and subdue it; and rule over the fish of the sea and over the birds of the sky and over every living thing that moves on the earth." [29]Then God said, "Behold, I have given you every plant yielding seed that is on the surface of all the earth, and every tree which has fruit yielding seed; it shall be food for you; [30]and to every beast of the earth and to every bird of the sky and to every thing that moves on the earth which has life, I have given every green plant for food"; and it was so. [31]God saw all that He had made, and behold, it was very good. And there was evening and there was morning, the sixth day. (Gen 1:24–31)

Question 25. What does the Bible say God made on the seventh day?

Answer: On the seventh day, God rested from His work *(a)*.

Scripture: Gen 2:1–2

(a) [1]Thus the heavens and the earth were completed, and all their hosts. [2]By the seventh day God completed His work which He had done, and He rested on the seventh day from all His work which He had done. (Gen 2:1–2)

Question 26. Who was the first man?

Answer: Adam was the first man *(a)*.

Scripture: Gen 2:20

(a) The man gave names to all the cattle, and to the birds of the sky, and to every beast of the field, but for Adam there was not found a helper suitable for him. (Gen 2:20)

Question 27. How was man created?

Answer: Man was created in the image of God *(a)* in righteousness and holiness *(b)*, with dominion over the creatures *(c)*.

Scripture: Eph 4:24, Gen 1:27, 28

(a) God created man in His own image, in the image of God He created him; male and female He created them. (Gen 1:27)

(b) And put on the new self, which in the likeness of God has been created in righteousness and holiness of the truth. (Eph 4:24)

(c) God blessed them; and God said to them, "Be fruitful and multiply, and fill the earth, and subdue it; and rule over the fish of the sea and over the birds of the sky and over every living thing that moves on the earth." (Gen 1:28)

Question 28. Did Adam remain perfect?

Answer: Adam fell from his perfect state by sinning against God *(a) (b) (c) (d)*.

Scripture: Gen 3:6, Eccl 7:29, Rom 3:23, 5:1

(a) When the woman saw that the tree was good for food, and that it was a delight to the eyes, and that the tree was desirable to make one wise, she took from its fruit and ate; and she gave also to her husband with her, and he ate. (Gen 3:6)

(b) Behold, I have found only this, that God made men upright, but they have sought out many devices. (Eccl 7:29)

(c) For all have sinned and fall short of the glory of God. (Rom 3:23)

(d) Therefore, just as through one man sin entered into the world, and death through sin, and so death spread to all men, because all sinned. (Rom 5:12)

Question 29. Did all mankind fall in Adam's first sin?

Answer: All mankind, descending from Adam, sinned in him, and fell with him in his first transgression *(a) (b) (c)*.

Scripture: 1 Cor 15:21–22, Rom 5:12, 18–19

(a) [21]For since by a man came death, by a man also came the resurrection of the dead. [22]For as in Adam all die, so also in Christ all will be made alive. (1 Cor 15:21–22)

(b) Therefore, just as through one man sin entered into the world, and death through sin, and so death spread to all men, because all sinned. (Rom 5:12)

(c) [18]So then as through one transgression there resulted condemnation to all men, even so through one act of righteousness there resulted justification of life to all men. [19]For as through the one man's disobedience the many were made sinners, even so through the obedience of the One the many will be made righteous. (Rom 5:18–19)

Question 30. Into what state did the fall bring mankind?

Answer: The fall brought mankind into a state of sin and misery *(a) (b) (c)*.

Scripture: Ps 51:5, Rom 5:18–19, Isa 64:6

(a) Behold, I was brought forth in iniquity, And in sin my mother conceived me. (Ps 51:5)

(b) [18]So then as through one transgression there resulted condemnation to all men, even so through one act of righteousness there resulted justification of life to all men. [19]For as through the one man's disobedience the many were made sinners, even so through the obedience of the One the many will be made righteous. (Rom 5:18–19)

(c) For all of us have become like one who is unclean, And all our righteous deeds are like a filthy garment; And all of us wither like a leaf, And our iniquities, like the wind, take us away. (Isa 64:6)

Question 31. Did God leave all mankind to perish in the state of sin and misery?

Answer: God, out of His good pleasure, saved His people from their sins through the redeemer, Jesus Christ *(a) (b) (c) (d)*.

Scripture: Jer 31:33, Matt 1:21, Rom 5:21, 2 Thess 2:13

(a) But this is the covenant which I will make with the house of Israel after those days," declares the LORD, "I will put My law within them and on their heart I will write it; and I will be their God, and they shall be My people. (Jer 31:33)

(b) She will bear a Son; and you shall call His name Jesus, for He will save His people from their sins." (Matt 1:21)

(c) So that, as sin reigned in death, even so grace would reign through righteousness to eternal life through Jesus Christ our Lord. (Rom 5:21)

(d) But we should always give thanks to God for you, brethren beloved by the Lord, because God has chosen you from the beginning for salvation through sanctification by the Spirit and faith in the truth. (2 Thess 2:13)

Question 32. What is sin?

Answer: Sin is disobeying God and His laws *(a)*.

Scripture: 1 John 3:4

(a) Everyone who practices sin also practices lawlessness; and sin is lawlessness. (1 John 3:4)

Question 33. What does every sin deserve?

Answer: Every sin deserves God's wrath and curse, both in this life *(a) (b) (c) (d),* and the next *(e).*

Scripture: Eph 5:6, Gal. 3:10, Prov 3:33, Ps. 11:6, Rev 21:8

- *(a)* Let no one deceive you with empty words, for because of these things the wrath of God comes upon the sons of disobedience. (Eph 5:6)

- *(b)* For as many as are of the works of the Law are under a curse; for it is written, "CURSED IS EVERYONE WHO DOES NOT ABIDE BY ALL THINGS WRITTEN IN THE BOOK OF THE LAW, TO PERFORM THEM." (Gal 3:10)

- *(c)* The curse of the LORD is on the house of the wicked, But He blesses the dwelling of the righteouss. (Prov 3:33)

- *(d)* Upon the wicked He will rain snares; Fire and brimstone and burning wind will be the portion of their cup. (Ps 11:6)

- *(e)* But for the cowardly and unbelieving and abominable and murderers and immoral persons and sorcerers and idolaters and all liars, their part will be in the lake that burns with fire and brimstone, which is the second death. (Rev 21:8)

Question 34. What are God's laws that he revealed to man?

Answer: God's law is the moral law, which is summarized in the Ten Commandments *(a).*

Scripture: Deut 10:4–5

- *(a)* [4]He wrote on the tablets, like the former writing, the Ten Commandments which the LORD had spoken to you on the mountain from the midst of the fire on the day of the assembly; and the LORD gave them to me. [5]Then I turned and came down from the mountain and put the tablets in the ark which I had made; and there they are, as the LORD commanded me. (Deut 10:4–5)

Question 35. What is the first commandment?

Answer: The first commandment is you shall have no other gods before Me *(a)*.

Scripture: Exod 20:3

  (a) You shall have no other gods before Me (Exod 20:3).

Question 36. What is the second commandment?

Answer: The second commandment is you shall not make any idol *(a)*.

Scripture: Exod 20:4

  (a) You shall not make for yourself an idol, or any likeness of what is in heaven above or on the earth beneath or in the water under the earth. (Exod 20:4)

Question 37. What is the third commandment?

Answer: The third commandment is you shall not take the Lord's name in vain *(a)*.

Scripture: Exod 20:7

  (a) You shall not take the name of the LORD your God in vain, for the LORD will not leave him unpunished who takes His name in vain. (Exod 20:7)

Question 38. What is the fourth commandment?

Answer: The fourth commandment is to remember the Sabbath day, and to keep it holy *(a)*.

Scripture: Exod 20:8

(*a*) Remember the Sabbath day, to keep it holy. (Exod 20:8)

Question 39. What is the fifth commandment?

Answer: The fifth commandment is to honor your father and mother *(a)*.

Scripture: Exod 20:12

(*a*) Honor your father and your mother, that your days may be prolonged in the land which the LORD your God gives you. (Exod 20:12)

Question 40. What is the sixth commandment?

Answer: The sixth commandment is you shall not murder.

Scripture: Exod 20:13

(*a*) You shall not murder. (Exod 20:13)

Question 41. What is the seventh commandment?

Answer: The seventh commandment is you shall not commit adultery *(a)*.

Scripture: Exod 20:14

(*a*) You shall not commit adultery. (Exod 20:14)

Question 42. What is the eighth commandment?

Answer: The eighth commandment is you shall not steal *(a)*.

Scripture: Exod 20:15

> *(a)* You shall not steal. (Exod 20:15)

Question 43. What is the ninth commandment?

Answer: The ninth commandment is you shall not bear false witness against your neighbor *(a)*.

Scripture: Exod 20:16

> *(a)* You shall not give false testimony against your neighbor. (Exod 20:16)

Question 44. What is the tenth commandment?

Answer: The tenth commandment is you shall not covet *(a)*.

Scripture: Exod 20:17

> *(a)* You shall not covet your neighbor's house; you shall not covet your neighbor's wife or his male servant or his female servant or his ox or his donkey or anything that belongs to your neighbor. (Exod 20:17)

Question 45. What is the sum of the Ten Commandments?

Answer: The sum of the Ten Commandments is to love the Lord our God with all our heart, with all our soul, with all our strength, and with all our mind; and to love our neighbor as ourselves *(a)*.

Scripture: Matt 22:37–40

(a) ³⁷And He said to him, YOU SHALL LOVE THE LORD YOUR GOD WITH ALL YOUR HEART, AND WITH ALL YOUR SOUL, AND WITH ALL YOUR MIND. ³⁸This is the great and foremost commandment. ³⁹The second is like it, YOU SHALL LOVE YOUR NEIGHBOR AS YOURSELF. ⁴⁰On these two commandments depend the whole Law and the Prophets. (Matt 22:37–40)

Question 46.   Is any man able perfectly to keep the commandments of God?

Answer: All men have sinned *(a) (b)* except one, Jesus Christ *(c)*.

Scripture: Rom 3:9, 23, 2 Cor 5:21

(a) What then? Are we better than they? Not at all; for we have already charged that both Jews and Greeks are all under sin. (Rom 3:9)

(b) For all have sinned and fall short of the glory of God. (Rom 3:23)

(c) He made Him who knew no sin to be sin on our behalf, so that we might become the righteousness of God in Him. (2 Cor 5:21)

Question 47. What is the penalty of Adam's sin?

Answer: The penalty for Adam's sin is death *(a) (b)*.

Scripture: Gen 2:17, Rom 6:23

(a) But from the tree of the knowledge of good and evil you shall not eat, for in the day that you eat from it you will surely die. (Gen 2:17)

(b) For the wages of sin is death, but the free gift of God is eternal life in Christ Jesus our Lord. (Rom 6:23)

Question 48. Does Adam's sin have on an effect on you?

Answer: Yes, we were born into sin, which causes death *(a)*.

Scripture: Rom 5:12

(a) Therefore, just as through one man sin entered into the world, and death through sin, and so death spread to all men, because all sinned. (Rom 5:12)

Question 49. Why does Adam's sin produce death for all mankind?

Answer: The guilt of Adam's sin was charged to all mankind, resulting in death *(a) (b)*.

Scripture: Rom 5:12–19, 1 Cor 15:22

(a) [12]Therefore, just as through one man sin entered into the world, and death through sin, and so death spread to all men, because all sinned [13]for until the Law sin was in the world, but sin is not imputed when there is no law. [14]Nevertheless death reigned from Adam until Moses, even over those who had not sinned in the likeness of the offense of Adam, who is a type of Him who was to come. [15]But the

free gift is not like the transgression. For if by the transgression of the one the many died, much more did the grace of God and the gift by the grace of the one Man, Jesus Christ, abound to the many. [16]The gift is not like that which came through the one who sinned; for on the one hand the judgment arose from one transgression resulting in condemnation, but on the other hand the free gift arose from many transgressions resulting in justification. [17]For if by the transgression of the one, death reigned through the one, much more those who receive the abundance of grace and of the gift of righteousness will reign in life through the One, Jesus Christ. [18]So then as through one transgression there resulted condemnation to all men, even so through one act of righteousness there resulted justification of life to all men. [19]For as through the one man's disobedience the many were made sinners, even so through the obedience of the One the many will be made righteous. (Rom 5:12–19)

(b) For as in Adam all die, so also in Christ all will be made alive. (1 Cor 15:22)

Question 50. How did Jesus Christ, being the Son of God, become man?

Answer: Jesus Christ was conceived by the Holy Spirit (a) and born of the virgin, Mary (b) (c).

Scripture: Matt 1:18, Isa 7:14, Luke 1:27

(a) Now the birth of Jesus Christ was as follows: when His mother Mary had been betrothed to Joseph, before they came together she was found to be with child by the Holy Spirit. (Matt 1:18)

(b) Therefore the Lord Himself will give you a sign: Behold, a virgin will be with child and bear a son, and she will call His name Immanuel. (Isa 7:14) *(c)* To a virgin engaged to a man whose name was Joseph, of the descendants of David; and the virgin's name was Mary. (Luke 1:27)

Question 51. How may we be saved from death?

Answer: We may be saved from death by grace alone through faith in Jesus Christ *(a)*.

Scripture: Eph 2:8–9

(a) [8]For by grace you have been saved through faith; and that not of yourselves, it is the gift of God; [9]not as a result of works, so that no one may boast. (Eph 2:8–9)

Question 52. Was Jesus Christ ever created?

Answer: Jesus Christ existed with God from all eternity *(a)*.

Scripture: John 1:1

(a) In the beginning was the Word, and the Word was with God, and the Word was God. 2He was with God in the beginning. (John 1:1)

Question 53. Did Jesus ever sin?

Answer: No, Jesus never sinned *(a)*.

Scripture: 2 Cor 5:21

(a) He made Him who knew no sin to be sin on our behalf, so that we might become the righteousness of God in Him. (2 Cor 5:21)

Question 54. For whom did Jesus die?

Answer: He died for His people *(a)*.

Scripture: Matt 1:21

> *(a)* She will bear a Son; and you shall call His name Jesus, for He will save His people from their sins. (Matt 1:21)

Question 55. What did Jesus' death on the cross accomplish?

Answer: Jesus' death on the cross accomplished forgiveness of our sins *(a) (b)*.

Scripture: Isa 53:4–5, Col 2:13–15

> *(a)* [4]Surely our griefs He Himself bore, And our sorrows He carried; Yet we ourselves esteemed Him stricken, Smitten of God, and afflicted. [5]But He was pierced through for our transgressions, He was crushed for our iniquities; The chastening for our well-being fell upon Him, And by His scourging we are healed. (Isa 53:4–5)

> *(b)* [13]When you were dead in your transgressions and the uncircumcision of your flesh, He made you alive together with Him, having forgiven us all our transgressions, [14]having canceled out the certificate of debt consisting of decrees against us, which was hostile to us; and He has taken it out of the way, having nailed it to the cross. [15]When He had disarmed the rulers and authorities, He made a public display of them, having triumphed over them through Him. (Col 2:13–15)

Question 56. What is saving faith?

Answer: Saving faith is believing on the Lord Jesus Christ unto eternal life *(a) (b) (c) (d) (e) (f) (g)*.

Scripture: John 1:12, 3:16, Acts 15:11, 16:31, 2 Cor 4:13, Gal 2:20, Eph 2:8

(a) But as many as received Him, to them He gave the right to become children of God, even to those who believe in His name. (John 1:12)

(b) For God so loved the world, that He gave His only begotten Son, that whoever believes in Him shall not perish, but have eternal life. (John 3:16)

(c) But we believe that we are saved through the grace of the Lord Jesus, in the same way as they also are. (Acts 15:11)

(d) They said, Believe in the Lord Jesus, and you will be saved, you and your household. (Acts 16:31)

(e) But having the same spirit of faith, according to what is written, "I BELIEVED, THEREFORE I SPOKE," we also believe, therefore we also speak. (2 Cor 4:13)

(f) I have been crucified with Christ; and it is no longer I who live, but Christ lives in me; and the life which I now live in the flesh I live by faith in the Son of God, who loved me and gave Himself up for me. (Gal 2:20)

(g) For by grace you have been saved through faith; and that not of yourselves, it is the gift of God. (Eph 2:8)

Question 57. What is justification?

Answer: Justification is the act of God when he pardons all our sins *(a) (b)*.

Scripture: Rom 3:24, Eph 1:7

(a) Being justified as a gift by His grace through the redemption which is in Christ Jesus; (Rom 3:24)

(b) In Him we have redemption through His blood, the forgiveness of our trespasses, according to the riches of His grace. (Eph 1:7)

Question 58. What is sanctification?

Answer: Sanctification is becoming more Christ-like through the work of the Holy Spirit *(a) (b) (c)*.

Scripture: Rom 6:11, Eph 4:24, 2 Thess 2:13

(a) Even so consider yourselves to be dead to sin, but alive to God in Christ Jesus. (Rom 6:11)

(b) And put on the new self, which in the likeness of God has been created in righteousness and holiness of the truth. (Eph 4:24)

(c) But we should always give thanks to God for you, brethren beloved by the Lord, because God has chosen you from the beginning for salvation through sanctification by the Spirit and faith in the truth. (2 Thess 2:13)

Question 59. What is the purpose of good works?

Answer: Good works are the fruits and evidences of a true faith *(a) (b)*.

Scripture: Jas 2:18, 22

(*a*) But someone may well say, "You have faith and I have works; show me your faith without the works, and I will show you my faith by my works." (Jas 2:18)

(*b*) You see that faith was working with his works, and as a result of the works, faith was perfected; (Jas 2:22)

Question 60. What happened to Jesus after He died on the cross?

Answer: Jesus rose from the dead *(a)*.

Scripture: Luke 24:36–43

(*a*) [36]While they were telling these things, He Himself stood in their midst and said to them, "Peace be to you." [37]But they were startled and frightened and thought that they were seeing a spirit. [38]And He said to them, "Why are you troubled, and why do doubts arise in your hearts?" [39]See My hands and My feet, that it is I Myself; touch Me and see, for a spirit does not have flesh and bones as you see that I have." [40]And when He had said this, He showed them His hands and His feet. [41]While they still could not believe it because of their joy and amazement, He said to them, "Have you anything here to eat?" [42]They gave Him a piece of a broiled fish; [43]and He took it and ate it before them. (Luke 24:36–43)

Question 61. What command did Jesus Christ give his followers before his ascension?

Answer: Jesus commanded his disciples to preach the gospel to all people *(a) (b)*.

Scripture: Matt 28:19–20, Mark 16:15

(a) [19]Go therefore and make disciples of all the nations, baptizing them in the name of the Father and the Son and the Holy Spirit, [20]teaching them to observe all that I commanded you; and lo, I am with you always, even to the end of the age. (Matt 28:19–20)

(b) And He said to them, Go into all the world and preach the gospel to all creation. (Mark 16:15)

Question 62. Who established the Church?

Answer: Jesus Christ established the Church *(a) (b) (c)*.

Scripture: Matt 16:18, 28:19–20, Mark 16:15

(a) I also say to you that you are Peter, and upon this rock I will build My church; and the gates of Hades will not overpower it. (Matt 16:18)

(b) [19]Go therefore and make disciples of all the nations, baptizing them in the name of the Father and the Son and the Holy Spirit, [20]teaching them to observe all that I commanded you; and lo, I am with you always, even to the end of the age. (Matt 28:19–20)

(c) And He said to them, Go into all the world and preach the gospel to all creation. (Mark 16:15)

Question 63. Who is the head of the Church?

Answer: Jesus Christ is the head of the Church *(a) (b) (c) (d)*.

Scripture: Matt 28:18–20, Eph 1:22, 5:23, Col 1:18

(a) ¹⁸And Jesus came up and spoke to them, saying, "All authority has been given to Me in heaven and on earth." ¹⁹ Go therefore and make disciples of all the nations, baptizing them in the name of the Father and the Son and the Holy Spirit, ²⁰teaching them to observe all that I commanded you; and lo, I am with you always, even to the end of the age." (Matt 28:18–20)

(b) And He put all things in subjection under His feet, and gave Him as head over all things to the church. (Eph 1:22)

(c) For the husband is the head of the wife, as Christ also is the head of the church, He Himself being the Savior of the body. (Eph 5:23)

(d) He is also head of the body, the church; and He is the beginning, the firstborn from the dead, so that He Himself will come to have first place in everything. (Col 1:18)

Question 64. What is the purpose of the Church?

Answer: The purpose of the Church is to worship *(a) (b)* the living God *(c)*.

Scripture: Ps 100, Matt 28:6, Phil 4:4

(a) ¹Shout joyfully to the LORD, all the earth. ²Serve the LORD with gladness; Come before Him with joyful singing. ³Know that the LORD Himself is God; It is He who has made us, and not we ourselves; We are His people and the sheep of His pasture. ⁴Enter His gates with thanksgiving And His courts with praise Give thanks to Him, bless His

name. [5]For the LORD is good; His lovingkindness is everlasting And His faithfulness to all generations. (Ps 100)

(b) Rejoice in the Lord always; again I will say, rejoice! (Phil 4:4)

(c) He is not here, for He has risen, just as He said. Come, see the place where He was lying. (Matt 28:6)

Question 65. What is the visible church?

Answer: The visible church is the gathering of professing believers *(a) (b) (c)*.

Scripture: Acts 2:42, 20:7, Eph 4:11,12

(a) They were continually devoting themselves to the apostles' teaching and to fellowship, to the breaking of bread and to prayer. (Acts 2:42)

(b) On the first day of the week, when we were gathered together to break bread, Paul began talking to them, intending to leave the next day, and he prolonged his message until midnight. (Acts 20:7)

(c) [11]And He gave some as apostles, and some as prophets, and some as evangelists, and some as pastors and teachers, [12]for the equipping of the saints for the work of service, to the building up of the body of Christ. (Eph 4:11–12)

Question 66. What is the invisible church?

Answer: The invisible church is the whole number of the elect, that have been, are, or shall be gathered into one under Christ *(a) (b) (c)*.

Scripture: John 10:16; 11:52, Eph 1:22–23

(a) I have other sheep, which are not of this fold; I must bring them also, and they will hear My voice; and they will become one flock with one shepherd. (John 10:16)

(b) And not for the nation only, but in order that He might also gather together into one the children of God who are scattered abroad. (John 11:52)

(c) ²²And He put all things in subjection under His feet, and gave Him as head over all things to the church, ²³which is His body, the fullness of Him who fills all in all. (Eph 1:22–23)

Question 67. What offices has Christ appointed in the church?

Answer: Christ has established overseers and deacons in the church *(a)*.

Scripture: Phil 1:1

(a) Paul and Timothy, bond-servants of Christ Jesus, To all the saints in Christ Jesus who are in Philippi, including the overseers and deacons. (Phil 1:1)

Question 68. What are the qualifications to be an overseer or deacon?

Answer: The qualifications to be an overseer or deacon are to be the husband of one wife, respectable, capable of teaching, gentle, and free from the love of money *(a)*.

Scripture: 1 Tim 3:2–10

(a) ²An overseer, then, must be above reproach, the husband of one wife, temperate, prudent, respectable, hospitable, able to teach, ³not addicted to wine or pugnacious, but gentle, peaceable, free from the love of money. ⁴He must be one who manages his own household well, keeping his children under control with all dignity ⁵(but if a man does not know how to manage his own household, how will he take care of the church of God?), ⁶and not a new convert, so that he

will not become conceited and fall into the condemnation incurred by the devil. [7]And he must have a good reputation with those outside the church, so that he will not fall into reproach and the snare of the devil. [8]Deacons likewise must be men of dignity, not double-tongued, or addicted to much wine or fond of sordid gain, [9]but holding to the mystery of the faith with a clear conscience. [10]These men must also first be tested; then let them serve as deacons if they are beyond reproach. (1 Tim 3:2–10)

Question 69. What two ordinances did Jesus Christ command?

Answer: Jesus Christ commanded baptism *(a)* and the Lord's supper *(b)*.

Scripture: Matt 28:19, 1 Cor 11:23–26

(a) Go therefore and make disciples of all the nations, baptizing them in the name of the Father and the Son and the Holy Spirit. (Matt 28:19)

(b) [23]For I received from the Lord that which I also delivered to you, that the Lord Jesus in the night in which He was betrayed took bread; [24]and when He had given thanks, He broke it and said, "This is My body, which is for you; do this in remembrance of Me." [25]In the same way He took the cup also after supper, saying, "This cup is the new covenant in My blood; do this, as often as you drink it, in remembrance of Me." [26]For as often as you eat this bread and drink the cup, you proclaim the Lord's death until He comes. (1 Cor 11:23–26)

Question 70. What is baptism?

Answer: Baptism is a sign of fellowship with Jesus Christ in his death, burial and resurrection *(a) (b) (c)*.

Scripture: Matt 28:19, Rom 6:3, Col 2:12

(a) Or don't you know that all of us who were baptized into Christ Jesus were baptized into his death? (Rom 6:3)

(b) Having been buried with Him in baptism, in which you were also raised up with Him through faith in the working of God, who raised Him from the dead. (Col 2:12)

(c) Go therefore and make disciples of all the nations, baptizing them in the name of the Father and the Son and the Holy Spirit. (Matt 28:19)

Question 71. What is the Lord's Supper?

Answer: The Lord's Supper is an ordinance consisting of bread and wine *(a) (b)*.

Scripture: 1 Cor 11:23–26, 1 Cor 10:16

(a) ²³For I received from the Lord that which I also delivered to you, that the Lord Jesus in the night in which He was betrayed took bread; ²⁴and when He had given thanks, He broke it and said, "This is My body, which is for you; do this in remembrance of Me." ²⁵In the same way He took the cup also after supper, saying, "This cup is the new covenant in My blood; do this, as often as you drink it, in remembrance of Me." ²⁶For as often as you eat this bread and drink the cup, you proclaim the Lord's death until He comes. (1 Cor 11:23–26)

(b) Is not the cup of blessing which we bless a sharing in the blood of Christ? Is not the bread which we break a sharing in the body of Christ? (1 Cor 10:16)

Question 72. What is Prayer?

Answer: Prayer is an offering up of our desires to God *(a)*, in the name of Christ *(b)*, with confession of our sin *(c)* and thankful acknowledgment of His mercy *(a)*.

Scripture: Phil 4:6, John 14:13–14, 1 John 1:9

(a) Be anxious for nothing, but in everything by prayer and supplication with thanksgiving let your requests be made known to God. (Phil 4:6)

(b) ¹³Whatever you ask in My name, that will I do, so that the Father may be glorified in the Son. ¹⁴If you ask Me anything in My name, I will do it. (John 14:13–14)

(c) If we confess our sins, He is faithful and righteous to forgive us our sins and to cleanse us from all unrighteousness. (1 John 1:9)

Question 73. What does the Bible promise about Jesus' return?

Answer: The Bible promises that Jesus will come a second time for all who believe *(a) (b)*.

Scripture: Heb 9:28, Acts 1:11

(a) So Christ also, having been offered once to bear the sins of many, will appear a second time for salvation without reference to sin, to those who eagerly await Him. (Heb 9:28)

(b) They also said, Men of Galilee, why do you stand looking into the sky? This Jesus, who has been taken up from you into heaven, will come in just the same way as you have watched Him go into heaven. (Acts 1:11)

Question 74. What will happen at Jesus' Second Coming?

Answer: Jesus Christ will judge the world in righteousness *(a) (b) (c)*.

Scripture: Acts 17:31, John 5:22, 27

(a) Because He has fixed a day in which He will judge the world in righteousness through a Man whom He has appointed, having furnished proof to all men by raising Him from the dead. (Acts 17:31)

(b) For not even the Father judges anyone, but He has given all judgment to the Son. (John 5:22)

(c) And He gave Him authority to execute judgment, because He is the Son of Man (John 5:27).

Question 75. What will happen to those that Jesus Christ deems righteous?

Answer: The righteous will receive eternal life, and an everlasting reward, in the presence of the Lord *(a) (b) (c)*.

Scripture: Matt 25:21, 34, 2 Tim 4:8

(a) His master said to him, 'Well done, good and faithful slave You were faithful with a few things, I will put you in charge of many things; enter into the joy of your master.' (Matt 25:21)

(b) Then the King will say to those on His right, 'Come, you who are blessed of My Father, inherit the kingdom prepared for you from the foundation of the world. (Matt 25:34)

(c) In the future there is laid up for me the crown of righteousness, which the Lord, the righteous Judge, will award to me

on that day; and not only to me, but also to all who have loved His appearing. (2 Tim 4:8)

Question 76. What will happen to those that Jesus Christ condemns?

Answer: The wicked that do not know God will be cast into everlasting torment *(a) (b)* and be separated eternally from God *(c)*.

Scripture: Matt 25:46, Mark 9:48, 2 Thess 1:7–10

(a) These will go away into eternal punishment, but the righteous into eternal life. (Matt 25:46)

(b) Where THEIR WORM DOES NOT DIE, AND THE FIRE IS NOT QUENCHED. (Mark 9:48)

(c) [7]and to give relief to you who are afflicted and to us as well when the Lord Jesus will be revealed from heaven with His mighty angels in flaming fire, [8]dealing out retribution to those who do not know God and to those who do not obey the gospel of our Lord Jesus. [9]These will pay the penalty of eternal destruction, away from the presence of the Lord and from the glory of His power, [10]when He comes to be glorified in His saints on that day, and to be marveled at among all who have believed—for our testimony to you was believed. (2 Thess 1:7–10)

Question 77. Why is there a final judgement?

Answer: The final judgement is appointed for the displaying of the glory of God's mercy, in the eternal salvation of the elect, and of his justice, in the eternal damnation of the wicked and disobedient *(a)*.

Scripture: Rom 9:22–23

> *(a)* [22]What if God, although willing to demonstrate His wrath and to make His power known, endured with much patience vessels of wrath prepared for destruction? [23]And He did so to make known the riches of His glory upon vessels of mercy, which He prepared beforehand for glory. (Rom 9:22–23)

Question 78.   What is hell?

Answer: Hell is a place of eternal fire and torment *(a)* for those who do not know God *(b)*.

Scripture: Luke 16:23–24; Matt 25:41

> *(a)* [23]In Hades he lifted up his eyes, being in torment, and saw Abraham far away and Lazarus in his bosom. [24]And he cried out and said, Father Abraham, have mercy on me, and send Lazarus so that he may dip the tip of his finger in water and cool off my tongue, for I am in agony in this flame. (Luke 16:23–24)

> *(b)* Then He will also say to those on His left, 'Depart from Me, accursed ones, into the eternal fire which has been prepared for the devil and his angels. (Matt 25:41)

Question 79.   What is heaven?

Answer: Heaven is where God dwells eternally *(a)*.

Scripture: Rev 21:1–22:5

> *(a)* [1]Then I saw a new heaven and a new earth; for the first heaven and the first earth passed away, and there is no longer any sea. [2]And I saw the holy city, new Jerusalem,

coming down out of heaven from God, made ready as a bride adorned for her husband. [3]And I heard a loud voice from the throne, saying, "Behold, the tabernacle of God is among men, and He will dwell among them, and they shall be His people, and God Himself will be among them, [4]and He will wipe away every tear from their eyes; and there will no longer be any death; there will no longer be any mourning, or crying, or pain; the first things have passed away." [5]And He who sits on the throne said, "Behold, I am making all things new "And He said, "Write, for these words are faithful and true." [6]Then He said to me, "It is done I am the Alpha and the Omega, the beginning and the end I will give to the one who thirsts from the spring of the water of life without cost." [7]He who overcomes will inherit these things, and I will be his God and he will be My son." [8]But for the cowardly and unbelieving and abominable and murderers and immoral persons and sorcerers and idolaters and all liars, their part will be in the lake that burns with fire and brimstone, which is the second death." [9]Then one of the seven angels who had the seven bowls full of the seven last plagues came and spoke with me, saying, " Come here, I will show you the bride, the wife of the Lamb."

The New Jerusalem

[10]And he carried me away in the Spirit to a great and high mountain, and showed me the holy city, Jerusalem, coming down out of heaven from God, [11]having the glory of God Her brilliance was like a very costly stone, as a stone of crystal-clear jasper. [12]It had a great and high wall, with twelve gates, and at the gates twelve angels; and names were written on them, which are the names of the twelve tribes of the sons of Israel. [13]There were three gates on the east and three gates on the north and three gates on the south and three gates on the west. [14]And the wall of the city had twelve foundation stones, and on them were the twelve names of the twelve apostles of the Lamb. [15]The one who spoke with

me had a gold measuring rod to measure the city, and its gates and its wall. [16]The city is laid out as a square, and its length is as great as the width; and he measured the city with the rod, fifteen hundred miles; its length and width and height are equal. [17]And he measured its wall, seventy-two yards, according to human measurements, which are also angelic measurements. [18]The material of the wall was jasper; and the city was pure gold, like clear glass. [19]The foundation stones of the city wall were adorned with every kind of precious stone The first foundation stone was jasper; the second, sapphire; the third, chalcedony; the fourth, emerald; [20]the fifth, sardonyx; the sixth, sardius; the seventh, chrysolite; the eighth, beryl; the ninth, topaz; the tenth, chrysoprase; the eleventh, jacinth; the twelfth, amethyst. [21]And the twelve gates were twelve pearls; each one of the gates was a single pearl And the street of the city was pure gold, like transparent glass. [22]I saw no temple in it, for the Lord God the Almighty and the Lamb are its temple. [23]And the city has no need of the sun or of the moon to shine on it, for the glory of God has illumined it, and its lamp is the Lamb. [24]The nations will walk by its light, and the kings of the earth will bring their glory into it. [25]In the daytime (for there will be no night there) its gates will never be closed; [26]and they will bring the glory and the honor of the nations into it; [27]and nothing unclean, and no one who practices abomination and lying, shall ever come into it, but only those whose names are written in the Lamb's book of life.

The River and the Tree of Life

[1]Then he showed me a river of the water of life, clear as crystal, coming from the throne of God and of the Lamb, [2]in the middle of its street On either side of the river was the tree of life, bearing twelve kinds of fruit, yielding its fruit every month; and the leaves of the tree were for the healing of the nations. [3]There will no longer be any curse; and the throne of God and of the Lamb will be in it, and

His bond-servants will serve Him; ⁴they will see His face, and His name will be on their foreheads. ⁵And there will no longer be any night; and they will not have need of the light of a lamp nor the light of the sun, because the Lord God will illumine them; and they will reign forever and ever (Rev 21:1 – 22:5).

Question 80. What is the duty, which God requires of man?

Answer: God requires man to obey His revealed will *(a) (b) (c) (d)*.

Scripture: Mic 6:8; Eccl. 12:13; Ps. 119:4; Luke 10:26–28

(a) He has told you, O man, what is good; And what does the LORD require of you But to do justice, to love kindness, And to walk humbly with your God? (Mic 6:8)

(b) The conclusion, when all has been heard, is: fear God and keep His commandments, because this applies to every person. (Eccl 12:13)

(c) You have ordained Your precepts, That we should keep them diligently. (Ps 119:4)

(d) ²⁶And He said to him, "What is written in the Law? How does it read to you?" ²⁷And he answered, "YOU SHALL LOVE THE LORD YOUR GOD WITH ALL YOUR HEART, AND WITH ALL YOUR SOUL, AND WITH ALL YOUR STRENGTH, AND WITH ALL YOUR MIND; AND YOUR NEIGHBOR AS YOURSELF." ²⁸And He said to him, "You have answered correctly; do this and you will live." (Luke 10:26–28)

Question 81. What is man's primary purpose?

Answer: Man's primary purpose is to glorify God *(a)* and to enjoy Him forever *(b)*!

Scripture: 1 Cor 10:31; Ps 73:25–26

(a) Whether, then, you eat or drink or whatever you do, do all to the glory of God. (1 Cor 10:31)

(b) 25Whom have I in heaven but You? And besides You, I desire nothing on earth. 26My flesh and my heart may fail, But God is the strength of my heart and my portion forever. (Ps 73:25–26)

Evening Prayer

Now I lay me down to sleep.
I pray the Lord my soul to keep.
If I should die before I wake,
I pray the Lord my soul to take.
Amen.

Morning Prayer

Now I awake and see the light,
'Tis God has kept me through the night;
To Him I lift my voice and pray,
That He will keep me through the day.
Amen.

The Lord's Prayer

Our Father, who art in heaven,
Hallowed be thy Name.
Thy kingdom come.
Thy will be done,
On earth as it is in heaven.
Give us this day our daily bread.
And forgive us our trespasses,
As we forgive those who trespass against us.
And lead us not into temptation,
But deliver us from evil.
For thine is the kingdom,
and the power,
and the glory,
for ever and ever.
Amen.

Made in the USA
Middletown, DE
26 September 2023

39456132R00031